i

A SALON OWNER'S GUIDE

Shear Business:

UNDERSTANDING THE ROLE YOU PLAY
IN THE BUSINESS YOU'RE CREATING

BY MELANIE FOOTE DAVIS

Foote-Davis, Melanie, 2008
A Salon Owner's Guide, Shear Business: Understanding The Role You Play In The Business You're Creating

ISBN **978-0-615-18929-1**

Cover Design: Designsbystacey@comcast.net
Salon Photo: Courtesy of Runway Studio
Headshot: Gerald Speight

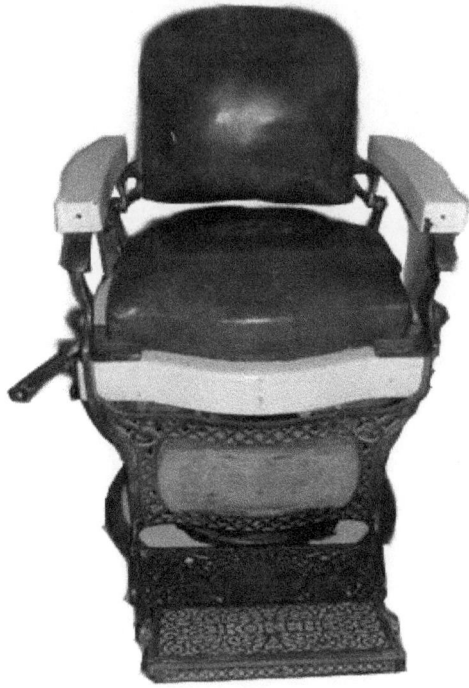

Pop Archie's Barber Chair

This book is dedicated to my father, Archie K. Foote, affectionately called "Pop Archie."

Dad, until recently, I never fully thought about the fact that we were in the same industry. I separated the two. To me you had a career as an electrician and a hobby, barbering. I didn't fully understand how you used the beauty industry to serve your community.

Dad you worked Friday evenings and all day Saturdays at your barbershop for over 60 years. It was a place of refuge for grandfathers, fathers and sons for camaraderie and grooming. Your prices were more than modest, practically free. When some didn't have the money to pay, they were never turned away.

As the years went by, some clients had lost almost every strand of hair on their heads. But they still dropped by to spend time with you, to shoot the breeze and reminisce about days gone by. Dad, you didn't stop there. You began to grow older and so did they. Some were no longer able to pay you a visit. What did you do? You went to their homes, to hospitals and to nursing homes to ensure that they were shaved and groomed.

Like most of those friends and clients, your barbershop no longer stands. What remains is soil rich in hopes, dreams and purpose. The sturdy old barber chair that now sits at home represents years of laughter, conversations and most importantly, love.

With that said, this is for you, Dad. I get it now, Dad! I now understand the lessons I was too stubborn to learn when I was younger. When I thought you were wasting your time with people who didn't pay, you knew what I didn't. It was your purpose to serve. Thank you for inspiring me to finish this project. May your spirit live in the hearts of others as well, as they too learn the **power behind the chair.**

Contents

Acknowledgements

Writing this book has been both challenging and rewarding.
I was led to do this by a power much greater than me. God
put this project in my heart. There were many days that
life's circumstances made it difficult for me to focus and
stay committed to seeing it come to fruition. Fortunately,
there are many people I hold close to my heart that made
completing this book possible. Special thanks to:

To my mother, Thelma Foote, you have taught me what it is
to be a woman of substance. Words will never express what
a joy it is to be your daughter. You helped me find my voice.
For this and so much more, I thank you.

Sean, my husband, my friend, I appreciate the efforts you
put toward keeping me sane when I felt like I was losing my
mind. You've stood beside me through difficult times.
You've honored your commitment to us by your actions.

Trinity, my beautiful daughter, I knew you were a jewel
before I ever held you. I had no idea how much of a blessing
you would be. As you grew, I also grew as a mother and as
a woman. God gave me the most precious gift when he gave
me you.

To my sisters, Beverly, Yvonne, Karen and Elaine, you offer
never-ending support with every endeavor I've pursued
without hesitation or judgment. We are family by God's
design. For this, I am grateful.

Thank you Bruce and Kevin for being my technical support,
for giving your opinions, encouragement and even your
corny jokes.

Chuck, thank you for your legal counsel.

Miki, knowing you is a gift in itself. I am grateful for your
guidance and honored to be your friend.

Anneke, Nia, Erica, LaMonica, Donna D, Donna W and other friends and family, there is safety in knowing that you're always there when I need you.

Mrs. Kelly, thank you the experience of working in a professional environment with a phenomenal team of artistic and incredible people.

Lyndsay, giving your time to edit and your honest recommendations are appreciated.

Shante, thank you for showing me what is possible.

Bridgette, I appreciate your encouragement and the use of your computer when I had no access.

To my life coach, Kally, you are a Godsend.

Thank you Tim for giving me my start.

To my clients, this journey would not have been the same without the opportunity to serve you.

Most importantly I thank you, **God,** for your unconditional love. God, you have shown me how awesome you are through the many miracles you've performed in my family and in my life. When I am obedient and allow you to guide me I prevail every time. I wouldn't be who I am without your grace, mercy and abiding love.

Introduction

The information in this book is based on my coaching knowledge, my experiences in the beauty industry and personal accounts from salon owners, stylists and clients. This guide is designed to increase the professionalism in an industry that I have been a part of most of my life. Take these tips, put them to good use and watch your business soar.

Imagine starting a business where the staff is excited about coming to work because they believe in you and your business. Now imagine what it would be like to have such great demand for your services that there's a waiting list to get an appointment. In addition to that, recruiting is not necessary because your database is full of talented artists wanting to work for you.

The good news is that **it's possible** to have what you want! I believe many salon owners start with enthusiasm and purpose. Many of them become stressed because they lose sight of their vision somewhere along the way. If you strongly believe in your vision and stay committed to your purpose, you will live to see it come to fruition.

This is not an opportunity for me to tell you what your business should be like. Instead, it is an opportunity for you to discover what type of salon you want to have. After all, it is your business. Therefore, you decide. My role is to help you clarify and remain true to your vision.

Each day you will have an opportunity to make choices. You have the choice to say yes or no. My wish is for you to clearly understand where each "yes" or "no" will lead your business. Your decisions will either create the business you want or the business you don't want. The added beauty is that these lessons will also be applicable in your personal life.

Chapter 1
It Begins With Me

Serenity Prayer: God grant me the serenity to accept the things I cannot change, the courage to change the things I can, and the wisdom to know the difference.
By Reinhold Niebuhr

Everything begins with you. Your attitude toward life influences the way you approach your business. Since your attitude is so important, it is necessary that you assess it often. The serenity prayer is a good assessment tool to help you recognize and embrace your responsibility for what happens in your life and your response to what happens.

Accept the things you cannot change. You cannot change time. You cannot change past business decisions. You cannot change what your competitors are doing. You cannot change the economy that influences your clients' spending.

Have the **courage** to change the things that can be changed. Have the courage to evaluate your current situation. Have the courage to take the necessary steps to create change. Have the courage to say "no" to things that could put your business in jeopardy. Your staff may not understand why you think change is important. So be willing to take that risk. Stay true to what is in the best interest of your business.

Wisdom: Be willing to recognize that which you have no control over. If you can't change it, accept that as fact and move on to what can be changed. You can change your hiring decisions. You can change your attitude. You can change the way you *respond* to others. You can change the way you spend your time with them. You can choose not to spend time with them at all. Although you may be able to influence people in some way, you can't *change* them. The changes others make are solely based on a personal decision to change.

Choices & Attitudes

When we're not careful, we can fall into the belief that we are victims of life's circumstances. We can believe that life just happens to us. The truth is we play a huge role in what happens to us. With every breath we take, we have an opportunity to choose.

Many people don't realize that we have so many choices to make. Some actions are "programmed" in our thoughts so we don't recognize them as choices. We conduct a huge portion of our daily activities on auto-plot. For example, many of us think we work because we have to work. It's actually a *choice.* We get up in the morning to go to work because we choose to do so.

Think of all the choices you make in a typical day. Most people eat when they feel hungry. Many beauty industry professionals continue to work until every client has been serviced. That's also a *choice.* Unfortunately, this is common practice in salons. It happens so often that it's become the culture of our business. "I'm going to lunch." are words you rarely hear in a salon.

Our intention is to take good care of the client. Our attitude suggests we have to choose one or the other. Try this option. Choose both. Choose to provide excellent service for your client *and* maintain your health. *Choose* to allow time to schedule a break for lunch *and* adequate time for each client. Preserve your health *and* work more efficiently.

Do you see the beauty of changing these attitudes and making new choices? Most beauty industry professionals work when they're sick. There aren't many salons that offer sick leave. Create an environment that promotes healthy living. Encourage the staff to have a balanced workday. Add scheduled lunches to your business model. As an owner you are raising awareness of the importance of health within the salon. You are contributing to your staff's well being while tending to your business. You are creating what you want. You want healthy staff. You want satisfied clients. How many other salons are offering that?

Choosing to properly schedule will allow adequate time to offer extra services to the clients scheduled for the day. And you will actually have time to make the client feel special without compromising your other appointments. It can generate more revenue for the artist and the business. At the end of the day, you've provided quality service to fewer clients. You've maintained your staff's health by working smarter not harder. You have satisfied clients. She will refer more clients because you honored her time.

Remember, **it begins with you**. Think about the current status of your business. Everything that is going on within your business today is the result of what you created yesterday. Think about the choices you made. Be conscious of the role you have played and will continue to play in business decisions.

It is your responsibility to create the business you want. It is your responsibility to make any changes you deem necessary. Accept it! Take ownership of that responsibility. Think about your attitude or beliefs. Did the situation just happen to you and your business? Did you allow it to happen?

Have the courage to make new choices. Have the courage to change your attitude. Know that you can create what you want. Choose to change what's not working well. Choose to keep what is working. Be willing to do something different. You can start from where you are at this very moment.

Current Business Status

What's working well for the business? List three (3) things are you pleased with.

1. _____
2. _____
3. _____

List three (3) things you are willing to accept.

1. _____
2. _____
3. _____

List three (3) things you are willing to change.

1. _____
2. _____
3. _____

What steps will you take to change these things?

1. _____
2. _____
3. _____

What will you do differently?

1. _____
2. _____
3. _____

List three (3) things you have no control over.

1. _____
2. _____
3. _____

Make the commitment. When will you begin?
Month_____Day_____Year_____

As of today, what will you say "Yes" to?

1. _____
2. _____
3. _____

Do you have anyone in your circle of influence to support you in this process? Name three. Contact them to tell how you need them to support you.

1. _____
2. _____
3. _____

I Am In Control of My Choices And My Attitude

Say "Yes"	Say "No"
• Business Vision	• Compromising Business
• Business Needs	• Tardiness
• Staying Focused	• Losing Focus
• Positive Attitude	• Negativity
• Self Reflection	• Selfishness
• Honoring Self	• Limitations
• Learning/Growth	• Flying Blind
• Setting Goals	• Hiring Blindly
• Sharing Knowledge	• Other's Drama
• Helping Others	• Spending Carelessly
• Smiling More	• Stress
• Letting Go	• Holding Other's Back

What Can I Control?

My Choices	My Attitudes
• What/who I listen to	• What I think of self
• What I say	• Be true to self
• What I learn	• Focus on positive
• Who I hire	• The way I respond
• How I hire	• Remain open to learn
• How I spend my time	• Avoid judging
• My actions	• Find good in others
• My spending habits	• Willing to give
• My activities	• Stay in gratitude

Chapter 2
Vision: What Do You See

When the thought of owning a salon crossed your mind you had an image of what it would be. For some of you the image may still be really vivid. For those of you who have been in business for a while that image may have faded or may be a little faint in your present state. You may even find that the image has been altered a bit. Like everything else in life, as you learn more about yourself you find that things you thought were important now have little or no significance. Nonetheless your vision started somewhere.

Let's do an exercise. Before we begin let's go over the rules. There are no right or wrong answers. It's your vision, not mine. What you see and how you see it is truly up to you. Let's begin. Go into a quiet place. Silence your cell phone. Turn off any background noise in the room. Lie on your back.

Take a few deep breaths. Breathe in deeply. Exhale. Inhale again. Exhale again. Repeat this several times until your feel your body relaxing. Close your eyes and imagine the most beautiful day you've ever experienced. The weather is perfect. Great things are happening in your life. You look amazing. You feel fabulous. It feels really good to be you. Now imagine walking towards your dream salon. What is the neighborhood like? Is it in a mall or shopping center? Do you own the building? How do you feel as you approach the entrance? Now walk through the doors of your dream salon. How is it decorated? What does it smell like? Is the aroma calming? Stop right there. Take a moment to breathe in the fragrance. How do you feel as you enter the salon? Does it feel warm and inviting? What colors do you see? What do those colors represent for you? How does it make you feel? How are you greeted? What is the concierge wearing? What does her hair and make-up look like? Picture the outfit? What's your impression of this person? When they greet you, how do you feel? Is the salon clean? Is there clutter anywhere? Are the retail shelves inviting? Does the retail display make you want to reach out and pick up an item and say, "Ooh what's this used for?" Is the waiting area quiet? Is it crowded? Is it noisy in the salon? Take a tour of the place. How big is it? Is there a spa? If so, where is it located? How does each area of the salon make you feel? What type of music do you hear? Is there a television? What do you see playing on the television? How are the stylists dressed? What are the clients like? How does your staff respond to you when they see you? Take a moment to take all of this in. Fully experience it. Enjoy this feeling. Say goodbye to your staff. Now open your eyes.

IT BEGINS WITH YOU

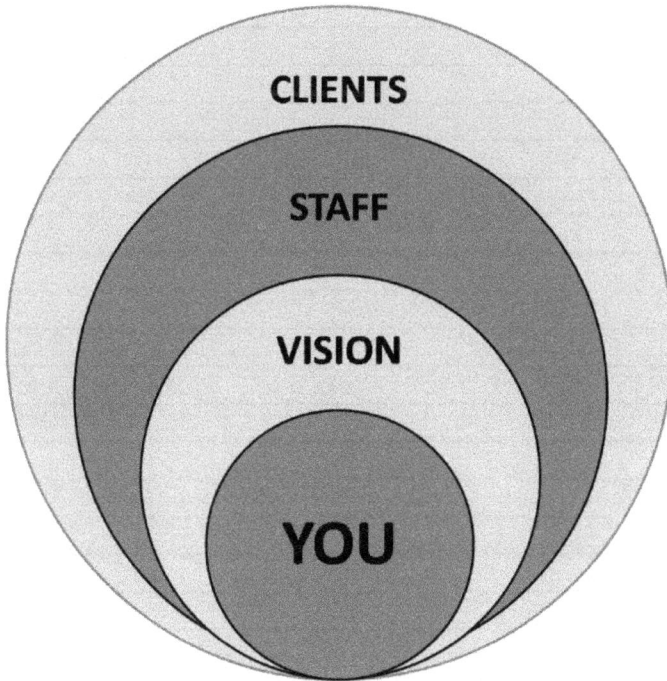

Take a moment to write down everything you can remember about your visit to your dream salon. Remember this is all about you. Write down whatever comes to mind. It does not have to make sense to anyone but you. Your vision is all yours. Your experience is your experience. What did you see? How did it feel? What was it like?

_____
_____
_____
_____
_____
_____
_____
_____
_____
_____
_____
_____
_____
_____
_____
_____
_____
_____
_____
_____
_____

The purpose of this exercise was for you to go back to where it all started with you. It's important for you to know what you want in order to get what you want. It may seem silly but this is the beginning of you having a clear understanding of how to structure your business. Many of your answers are found in the visioning exercise. If your business gets stressful it may be because you've compromised your vision. As we continue, it's vitally important for you to hold that vision. Remember that **you play a significant role in creating whatever takes place in your business.**

Key things to remember: When you say, "Yes" to one thing you're saying "No" to something else. In essence, when you say, "No" to your vision you're saying "Yes" to someone else's.

Key questions to ask: Is this in the best interest of my business? Why or Why not?

Is this in alignment with my vision?

Defining Your Vision

Let's talk about your reason for choosing this business and create a mission statement based on that.

The mission statement should be clear so you and your staff are able to fully understand the meaning and purpose for your business.

Be as specific as possible. Keep in mind that you can always go back and make changes. We are constantly evolving. As you learn more about who you are and what you want, you may change the direction of your business.

- Describe your target market?
- Demographics (age, economic status, etc.)
- What is the culture of your business?
- Why would clients choose your business?
- What should clients expect?
- What makes you unique?
- Are there any social or moral issues that you value?
- Do you want your business to reflect your values?
- What do you want to be known for?
- What is your desired geographical location?
- Describe your services?
- How much would you like to profit annually?

Think about the questions. Answer the questions. Think about your reason for being in business. Now write a brief statement. Describe who you are. State what your business represents. State what you will provide for your clients.

_____

_____

_____

_____

_____

_____

_____

_____

_____

Target market

_____
_____
_____
_____

Every business has a culture. We generally eat popcorn and
dress casual when we go to a movie theatre. People dress
up when they go to the opera. Celebrities dress up for the
Academy Awards. The attire is more relaxed for the
Billboard Awards. It's the culture of the business. It's the
way things are done in that business.. What is the way you
do things in your business? What is the culture your
business?

_____
_____
_____
_____

What is your brand? What do you want people to think of
when they hear your name?

_____
_____
_____
_____

What makes your business unique?

_____
_____
_____
_____

What social or moral issues are important to you?

_____
_____
_____
_____

Do you want your business to reflect these values? Circle
One **Yes** or **No**

There are a few other things that must be aligned with your vision.

Salon Image

There are many factors that play a role in the image of your business. The way you carry yourself, the people you hire, and the mannerisms of the team and the marketing materials you distribute are all an important part of the salon image. The furniture and design of the business make a statement. Select a dress code that reflects the type of business you want to attract. Determine the type of music you want to play. All of this helps to create an atmosphere. The atmosphere will dictate the behaviors within the doors of your business.

Professionalism

The word professional is like the word success. It may mean different things to different people. If we want to be recognized as a respectable profession, we must demonstrate respectable qualities. If we want to charge top dollar, we need to provide top service!

Would you expect the server to talk on her cell phone while taking your order at a five star restaurant? What makes you think someone wants to pay you for that type of service or shall I say lack of customer service? Are you willing to pay for an unclean hotel room with dirty sheets? Then why would you expect someone to pay you for a station that's just plain nasty? Would you pay your doctor to eat while performing surgery? Why would you expect someone to pay you for eating Buffalo wings at your station?

I guess you're beginning to get an idea of what my definition of professionalism is. When we walk into other businesses we've learned to expect certain behaviors. What do you want clients to expect when they walk through the doors of your business?

This is your vision! This is your business! This all ties into what you want for your business and how you want people to view your business.

Let's use the movie or television industry as a vignette for your business. Salon owners, like many small business owners, tend to wear many hats. You are the screenwriter, the director and the producer. The script you write will define how your business is run. The actors you cast will be those you hire to work in your business.

Take a moment to define what professionalism is according to you. Be specific. Here are a few questions to get you started on your script. This is also connected to defining the roles of the characters in your movie.

What is the telephone greeting for your business?
Example: "Welcome to Ambiance Studio of Design. How may I help you?"

What is the greeting when someone walks through your doors?

How do you want your staff to dress?
Example: all black, black & white, salon t-shirts with black slacks. Are hats allowed in the salon? Are jeans and sneakers permitted?

How do you want your staff to behave? Do you want them focused on the client in the chair or conversing with the artist next to them?

What are the business hours?

Are the appointments and client records kept electronically?

Do you offer client consultations for all new clients or services? This is highly recommended.

What type of products are you going to retail? What do these products say about you and your business?

What types of services do you provide?

What's the cost of each service?

Who are your competitors? What are your competitors providing that you aren't?

What makes your business unique? What one thing can you do to make your business stand out?
Does everyone have the same business cards? (I recommend it to look more uniform)

Is continued education a criterion to work at your establishment?

Does your business provide free training?

What forms of payment do you accept? (credit cards, cash, checks)

Do you allow solicitors in your place of business? Is it okay with you that Tony's selling bootleg DVD's in your establishment?

How clean is your business? Do you have a cleaning service? What's the staff's role in this process?

How is each station left at the close of business each day? Do you want each station to look uniform at the end of the day?

Do you offer vacation? How is vacation time or requested days off managed and communicated?

What holidays will the business be closed?

Do you offer insurance?

Which staff members will have keys to your establishment?

The Power Of A Vision

Let me tell you a short story about a salon owner with a well-defined vision. In the beginning she hired based on her vision or mission statement. There was a certain image she wanted her stylist to have.

Technical skills were important. But it was extremely important for the staff to be able and willing to play the role. The artists were expected to dress in the latest fashion. They were expected to be on time. They were expected to attend all staff meetings. The salon owner provided training. She also expected the artists to continue their own education.

The boundaries were crystal clear. She hired only those who met the criteria for her business. This owner knew what she wanted. She built a fabulous team. I am not using the word team lightly. This team worked well together. It was a fascinating production to watch. The entire team had a fully committed book.

Business was booming! Things were going so well. The owner serviced clients at her leisure. She vacationed regularly fully confident that the salon would run efficiently in her absence. The business made money. The team made money. The clients enjoyed patronizing this salon. The salon owner had created a win: win for all parties involved.

Several years later something changed. The opportunity for growth within the salon no longer exists. One by one, the artists began to resign.
It was time for them to venture out to pursue other endeavors. The salon owner had difficulty accepting this reality. This transition was something she had not anticipated. Unbeknownst to her, she had become too cozy in her comfort zone.

Devastated and desperate, she made an attempt to build a new team. She began to hire for reasons other than what was best for her business. The new people were not motivated. The culture of the business changed drastically. The salon owner sold the business and moved on.

What do you think happened? What changed? The salon owner lost sight of her vision. She didn't understand that she had the power to recreate another win:win situation. She adopted the attitude of a victim. Her vision was no longer visible.

Do you see how important it is to hold the vision? Do you understand how much power there is in your choices and your attitudes? She said, "Yes" to playing the role of a victim. She said "No" to taking control of her business. Take ownership of your business! Hire based on your vision.

Chapter 3
Defining Roles

What can they expect from you? What are your expectations for them? It is crucial that every character you cast knows and understands their role. Always set the expectations for your staff. Never assume they understand what you want or expect from them. Clearly define what you want. For example: Demonstrate how you want the phones to be answered. What is your official greeting? Demonstrate how you want the clients greeted. If you want them to walk up to the client, shake her hand, introduce themselves then by all means demonstrate it. Be as specific and as detailed as possible. Explain what you want the client's experience to be from the first point of contact with your business to the completion of the service. The first point of contact may mean when the client calls for an appointment or when she enters as a walk-in. If you expect the client's service to include escorting her to the door, state that. Leave no stone unturned. It will save you a great deal of stress from misunderstandings later. Be as specific as possible in every aspect of your business. Define every role for every cast member.

Develop a salon handbook for your business. Make sure that every cast member receives one the day they're hired. Have them read it and sign that they have read and understand the policies and requirements to maintain employment. Now each cast member has a script to use to ensure the entire cast is communicating the same message when speaking to clients.

Define each role in your business on a separate sheet. Be as specific as possible in the job description. Keep in mind that not all managers are stylists. Include what you expect from them.

Be clear about the chain of command so that concerns and issues are directed to the appropriate command person. Who does she call in case of an emergency? Who is responsible for client issues?

Feel free to change the title to whatever is suitable for your business. Have fun with it. Be as creative as you like.

Owner:
Director/Manager:
Assistant Director/Assistant Manager
Artistic Director:
Front Desk Coordinator:
Color Specialist:
Senior Stylist:
Junior Stylist:
Lead Shampoo Assistant:
Shampoo Assistant:
Spa Director
Massage Therapist
Aesthetician
Nail Technician
Barber

Chain of Command

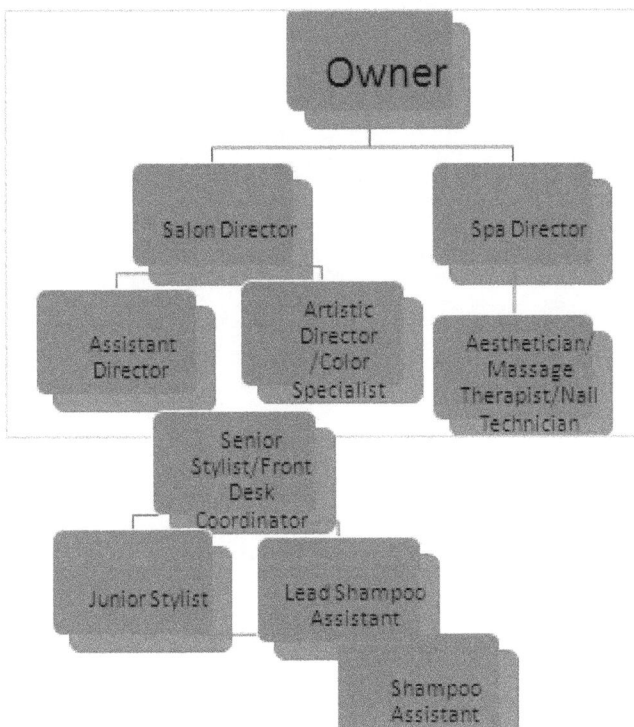

Chapter 4
Casting Call For Success: Scripting Your Business

Think of your business as a movie, play or television series. Your script is your business plan. The casting call is the process of looking for staff. The interviewing process is your audition. The characters are the people you hire. The clients that visit your salon are the extras.

Consider these things when you're creating your business. Think about the script for your salon. Cast the characters based on the theme of your project. Will you produce a movie called "Pimp Dat Weave", "Curl It Like It's Hot", "Ambiance" or "The Artist Design Studio"?

Keep in mind that the clients who are extras have *multiple roles.* These clients are also your viewers, your critics and your advertisement. Everyone the existing clients have contact with is a potential client or your potential audience. They will decide to tune in to your television series or buy a ticket for your movie based on the reviews of the critics and the advertisements of the existing clients.

Your movie will not be a box office hit or earn you an academy award nomination if you do not appropriately cast the right characters. Your television series will not remain on the air for another season if the ratings are bad. Good reviews are inevitable when you hold the vision, cast appropriately and each character knows their lines.

How are salons, especially African-American salons, portrayed in movies? Full-fledged drama is what I see! The stylists are catty. There is gossip with clients and about clients. Is that what you want? Do you want people to have low expectations of you and your business?

It's not too late to change the stereotype of our industry. Remember it begins with you. We literally touch a lot of people in this business. Be mindful that there is power in touch. You are in an industry that is licensed to do just that, touch. Aside from the medical field who else has that authority? The way you do business is something you have the power to change.

Lights, Camera, Action

Pretend the cameras are always rolling. The film industry's goal is to create a buzz about an upcoming movie. You want to create a buzz about your new salon. The buzz about this hot new salon will have people calling to schedule an appointment.

Onstage vs. Offstage

Your cast members need to understand that they are to follow the script whenever they're onstage. Let's define what's considered onstage. Onstage is whenever clients are present. If the client is anywhere in the building the script is in play. That means even when you think the client is out of earshot or not paying attention. If the client is in the restroom, you're onstage. If the client is on her cell phone and she appears to be engrossed in an important conversation, you're still onstage.

What's not in the script? Gossip, talking about an issue you're having with the owner, discussing what you did last night with your significant other, discussing your paycheck, etc

What's in the script? Client consultations, making sure the client is comfortable, a plan of action for the client's future appointments, retail for them to take home, asking for referrals etc.

Offstage can be defined as staff meeting, before opening, after closing, in a private meeting with the manager/owner or when you're on break away from the salon.

Staff Meetings: Dress Rehearsals

Staff meetings serve as your dress rehearsals. I encourage you to have regularly scheduled staff meetings. It allows you and your cast to openly and effectively communicate any challenges or issues that can affect the business. It's also a good time to ensure that the entire cast is informed of any edits in your script. Script edits include trainings, salon promotions, policy changes and updates that are important to the business operations.

Staffing: Casting Your Characters

The business will not function effectively without the right characters cast for your script. When you choose to cast someone for your production be sure they will appeal to your audience. In other words hire based on your vision. What do I mean by that? Find out whom you're hiring. Get to know the whole person. Ask questions that describe how they think, feel and how they operate. Learn about their lifestyle and interests. An actress tends to draw from her own life experiences to tap into the emotions needed for a specific scene. In the same way, a stylist may conduct business based on her life experiences.

Those you hire are people with real dreams. Our industry is full of gifted, creative and resourceful people. We are artists. Our unique perspective is often reflected in the work we do. Embrace that during each audition. Keep this in mind during the hiring process.

I've listed sample questions to ask during an interview. Notice that the questions are not based on technical skills. I am not discounting the significance of those skills. However, the thought process or mindset of the artist is critical to the image of your business. Not to mention your profit margin. Attitude can literally cost you your business.

Sample Interview Questions

What are your dreams?

What's important to you?

What made you choose this industry?

What's fascinating about this industry?

What do you like least about this industry?

What attracted you to this salon? Why did you choose to apply to work here?

What do you enjoy most?

What do you enjoy the least?

What motivates you?

What would you like your work environment to feel like? Look like?

How do you plan to build your clientele?

How often do you see your clients?

How do you track clients' records?

Why do you feel clients come to you?

Tell me about your ideal boss/manager.

Do you know how much money you made last year?

How much do you want to make this year?

What is your ideal work situation?
What do you feel is the key reason for your success?

Have you ever worked in sales?

What was the last book you read?

What's your favorite movie? Why?

Situational questions

What does the word "TEAM" mean to you?

Tell me about a time when you were a good team player.

Give me an example of a difficult client and how you
handled it?
Difficult teammate?

Tell me about your ideal teammates.

Have you ever assisted other stylists?

How well do you receive feedback/constructive criticism?

How well do you give feedback/constructive criticism? Give
me an example of how you would give feedback to an
associate.

Tell me about a hair show you attended. How did you spend
your time?

The salon opens at 9am. Your 1st client is 10:30am. What
time do you arrive?

If you were booked for the week, your client really
needs/wants to come in, what would you do?

When you're on vacation or it's your off day, where do your
clients go to be serviced?
What was the last class you took?

What do you do well?

What do you feel you need to improve?

Do you prefer commission or booth rent?

31

Which position is more important: stylist, owner, salon assistant, or the front desk coordinator? Please explain.

What days & hours are you available to work?

When are you able to begin employment?

Is it ok for me to contact your previous employer?

On a scale of 1-10 (1=least important 10=most important)
How important is client retention? Why/why not?

How important is retail? Why/why not?

How important are staff meetings? Why/why not?

How important is continuing education?

Revelations and Teachable Moments
There is more to a person than the skills they possess. Notice the discoveries you may have during an audition. Let's take a look at why this is important to the success of your business. Read the questions. Then look at what it could possibly reveal. You may also discover a few teachable moments and find the need to edit your script.

What are your dreams? This will show you how broad her vision is. This lets you know how open she is to new things.

What's fascinating about this industry? This tells you where her interests lie. You may be able to support her with her goals in the industry based on this information. If she's fascinated with color, she could become your Color Design Specialist. If she likes competitions, she could be your Award Winning Stylist. The possibilities are endless. Your support can be great for her confidence, her loyalty to the business and great marketing for your business.

What would keep you from showing up for work? This is a strong indicator of what's important to her. This tells you what she's committed to and what her priorities are.

What motivates you? This will tell you how to inspire her. Some people are motivated by recognition. Some like to feel appreciated. Others are motivated by money, titles, power etc. Pay close attention. Listen for the clues.

How do you plan to build your clientele? This will tell you if she's self-motivated. Does she hold herself responsible for her own growth or does she consider that to be your job?

How often do you see your clients? Weekly? 2weeks? 4 weeks? 6-8 weeks? Does she understand the importance of client retention?

How do you track clients' records? Is she organized? Client history is important for many reasons. Even if you do have a great memory, why would you want the responsibility of keeping your entire clientele's service records in your head? Would you want your doctor to depend on memory to track your medical history? It's important to document how a client responds to the products we use. If the result from the product was less than desirable, document it for future reference. If the stylist is away from the salon another stylist can know exactly what to do. This is a great way to build trust in your team. They can have the confidence of knowing that the client will be taken care of in the event of an emergency or whatever the reason is for her absence. It makes for a positive client experience. It builds the clients' trust in the salon. The client will be less likely to take her business elsewhere.

Why do you think clients come to you? This lets you know if she is aware of her gifts. Does she actively listen to her clients' needs? Does she take the time to know her clients as people or does she see them as just dollar signs? Does she refer to the client as, "my five o'clock client" or does she know her name? I feel that one of the ways I built my clientele was because they liked me as a person. I listened to them. I helped them to feel better about themselves. I cared about them as an individual. They may have been able to go somewhere else and get better haircut. They sat in my chair because I helped them feel like they were important. They *are* important. Understand the gift in treating each client as if she's the only client in the world.

Tell me about your ideal boss/manager. This is her way of telling you what she expects of you. Listen carefully to the spoken and the unspoken.

How much do you want to make this year? Is she a goal setter? She needs a guide to measure her financial success.

Do you know how much money you made last year? Is she measuring her success or just living each day with no sense of purpose? Living without a goal is like running a race not knowing where the finish line is. How can you measure how far you've got to go if you don't know where you're going?

What is your ideal work environment or situation? This expresses how she views the industry. You'll hear clues for her professionalism and how her environment has influenced her expectations of the beauty industry.

What do you feel is the key reason for your success? Let's you know how she defines success.

Have you ever worked in sales? This is a sales business! You're selling services, products, your business and yourself. If she doesn't understand that, this may highlight a teaching opportunity. If you choose to hire her you can teach her how to generate more income for herself and the business by offering additional services or up selling.

What was the last book you read? This may tell you what she's interested in and what she's passionate about. Understanding her passion will give you clues about how to motivate her.

What does the word "TEAM" mean to you? We don't all view our roles on a team the same way. This provides more clarity on her perspective of a team.

Tell me about a time when you were a good team player. Gives you an example of what type of player you have on your team. What role will she play?

Give me an example of a difficult client or teammate and how you handled it? This makes you aware of what conflict resolutions skills she has, if any. Will she create more drama or diffuse it?

Have you ever assisted other stylists? This is another example of whether she's a team player or not. We all depend on the assistance of another being in some way, shape or form. Here's an example. Toni has Ms. Jones in her chair. Ms. Jackson is waiting to be styled by Toni. Ms. Smith is waiting to be blow-dried. And there is one new client waiting to see Toni for a consultation. Needless to say, Toni is running behind schedule or possibly over-booked. Michael has one client under the dryer and no one waiting. How beautiful would it be for Michael to offer to blow dry Ms. Smith? Ms. Smith will be happy because she's closer to finishing and walking out of the door. She'll also remember how supportive Michael was. Ms. Smith may even refer clients to him because she appreciates his efforts. Toni is appreciative of the help. That reduces the waiting time for all of the clients. It doesn't take Michael away from his client under the dryer. He feels good about his small yet memorable contribution. The new client gets to see how well the staff works together. What a great first impression!

How well do you receive feedback/constructive criticism? This is a very sensitive area. It's an opportunity for growth. Feedback is designed to encourage more positive behavior or to enhance a skill or technique. Her response will give you an indication of her ability to grow. It will also demonstrate her thoughts about accountability and responsibility for her actions.

How well do you give feedback/constructive criticism? Give me an example of how you would give feedback to an associate. Is she able to be tactful and respectful?

Tell me about a hair show you attended. How did you spend your time? If the most important thing to her was getting "good deals" on products, purses, jewelry and partying, pay attention. Think about it. Is that aligned with your business model? To be clear asks more questions. Suppose she seems really excited about what she learned and how it helped her to grow. Consider how that is aligned with your business model.

The salon opens at 9am. Your first client is 10:30am. What time do you arrive? This question shows her perception of how she fits into the larger picture. Staff should be available when the salon doors open. Let's explore this for a moment. The salon opens at 9:00 am. The first appointment for the day is not scheduled until 10:30am. For example, your policy states that stylists are not required to arrive until their first scheduled appointment. There is a walk-in at 9:15am. Who's there to service the walk-in clients? Ask yourself, what is the perception of you and your business if this happens? How does this fit into your business model? Is this in alignment with your vision or not? How much will this situation cost you? Be very careful with how you structure your business. What and whom were you saying yes to when you made this agreement? Was this scheduling decision in the best interest of your business? Evaluate this. It may be a great time to edit your script.

If you were booked for the week, but your client, Sharon Jacobs, really needs/wants to come in, what would you do? Her response will tell you if her priority is taking care of the need of the client or her own personal needs. Let me explain. If she refers the client to another teammate who is available at the requested appointment time, her priority is servicing the client. If she over-books to accommodate the client, then she may honestly think that her priority is servicing the client. Based on her way of thinking, she believes this is the best way to service her client.

From a business standpoint, the best choice would be referring her client to a teammate. Scheduling several clients within an hour creates a domino effect. Once you squeeze that person in, you've just increased the chances of running late for your other clients. Is that fair to those clients? The truth is, overbooking diminishes the level of service a stylist is able to provide to the clients that are already scheduled to see her. It was well intended, however the results cause an adverse effect.

In order for us to be more professional and provide better customer service, we must change our way of thinking. What is the harm in referring that client to a fellow teammate? What's the gift in it? "Ms. Jacobs, I know how important it is for your hair to look fabulous for your meeting. However, I'm fully committed for the week. Michael is available at your requested appointment time. I'm sure that he'll take good care of you. Let's move forward with scheduling you to see Michael." You'll be right there if Michael has any questions. You can remain on schedule for the other clients. Ms. Jacobs looks fabulous. The business didn't lose the revenue. Michael is glad to be on your team. There are great rewards in being the "back-up stylist." Many junior stylists build their clientele playing back up/understudy. (The understudy is the person who learns all of the lines for a role. If the actor for that part gets sick or something the understudy can easily play the role.)

When you're on vacation or it's your off day, where do your clients go to be serviced? Again her response will reveal the same mindset as the previous question. To accommodate as many clients as possible, many stylists work longer hours prior to leaving town. This is fine when she is able to provide the best service. However, when it begins to minimize the level of service the client receives, encourage her to refer the clients to her teammates. The client doesn't have to find another salon to be serviced during her absence. If there are any questions about which products were used on prior visits, the records are right there. The revenue does not walk out the door to the salon down the street. It demonstrates unity within the business. How cool is that?

Her response to the last two (2) will demonstrate her ability to be flexible or resourceful when presented with a dilemma while keeping the client's best interest in mind.

How often do you take classes? What/when was the last class you took? What skills do you feel you need to work on? How much does she value continued education? How serious is she about her craft? It will also tell you if she is teachable. If you have a know-it-all on your team she won't be open to learning and growing. This will possibly add to your daily frustrations in the salon.

Do you prefer commission or booth rent? Why? If she feels strongly about something other than what's written in your script then you may not have a role for her to play. Listen to her explanation. Transitioning into a new role may be why she's at the audition.

Which position is more important: stylist, owner, salon assistant or the front desk coordinator? Please explain. This is an indication of how she values her teammates. Does she see herself as the "Leading Actress"? Every role is vital to the survival of the salon. Each role is in support of the other. You need supporting actors unless your production is a one-woman show.

What days & hours are you available to work? Is she available to during the hours that are conducive to your business needs? If not are you willing to make accommodations to support her needs? What are you saying yes to? Is this in the best interest of your business? Some circumstances call for different measures. This may be one of them. Decide accordingly. Be clear on what and why you made the agreement.

Would your previous employer hire you again? Why or why not? Is it ok for me to contact your previous employer? This may tell you if she left on positive terms.

Does she burn bridges? Is it always someone else's fault? Is she always the victim? It's not important that you know the specifics of her past situation. Listen carefully to the response. Watch the body language. Look for clues.

I'm going to say this again. Find out who you're hiring. Get to know the whole person. Ask questions that describe what they think, how they feel, and how they do things. Learn about their lifestyle and interests. Please understand that this will tell you who is going to show up for work on a daily basis. Many have mastered the skill of interviewing. The truth is the attitude they have about life is the attitude that will come to the salon. Remember who you hire is a reflection of you and your business. The questions you ask during the interview phase are very important. The things you look for during the interview are very important. The signs are almost always there. Knowing how to identify the signs during the interview process is crucial. There is a saying, "When people show you who they are, believe them."

Example: She shows up late for the interview without calling ahead. Chances are she is not going to show up for work on time either. Does this mean that she's always late? Of course not, this may be an isolated event. Do you need to address time during the interview? Absolutely, if time is something you value. Make a decision after carefully listening to the response.

Example: Her interview attire is more appropriate for going to the fitness center. Chances are her work attire may not be in alignment with your dress code. Maybe the salon she previously worked in had a relaxed dress code. Therefore she was unaware of your idea of interview attire. If her attire causes your hair to stand on the back of your neck, be sure to address this concern during the interview. If her attire doesn't bother you, move on. It's your vision. It's your business. **You get to create the environment.**

Let's be fair. Her responses to your interview questions may not meet your level of expectations. Be mindful of the fact that we all come from different backgrounds. Therefore, we must not treat people differently or perceive their way of doing things as inferior because it is different. She may or may not have had the same exposure to your business cultures. Maybe this is an opportunity to share new information with her.

On a scale of 1-10 (1=least important 10= most important)
How important is client retention? Why/why not? New clients are good to have. The goal is to convert new clients into regular clients. Client retention is the bulk of your revenue. Period.

How important is retail? Why/why not? This tells you if she understands the value in retail. May present another opportunity to educate. Clients need products to maintain the care of the hair, skin and nails between visits. Why send them to a beauty supply store or another salon when they can buy from you? Using salon exclusive products keeps clients out of local drug stores and beauty supply stores.

How important are staff meetings? Why/why not? This gives you a heads-up on if they will show up for staff meetings with a positive attitude or not. You may need to educate them on why meetings are important to the team and the survival of the business.

Once the applicant is gone. While the information you've collected is still fresh on your mind. Take a minute to examine your thoughts. Answer to the following questions:

1.Does she appear to be teachable?

2.Is her attitude about life so far from yours that you feel like working with her will deplete your energy? If the answer is yes, don't hire her.

3. Was your vision just new to her?

4. Was there a positive shift in her body language when you introduced your business concept? If yes, then you may want to consider casting her for a role in your production.

5. Is her attitude in alignment with your vision for the business or your mission statement?

6. What is she bringing to the team? List three qualities or skills she possesses that make her an asset.

_____

_____

_____

7.Is she a possible liability? If yes, what are the liabilities?

_____

_____

_____

8. Are the liabilities worth the business risk? Why?

_____

_____

_____

9. What red flags do you see? Hopefully you won't see any. If you do see red flags, do not ignore them? Again, I warn you if you see red flags identify them. Ask yourself, "Is the liability worth the business risk?" How much could it possibly cost me in time, stress, aggravation and money? Is it really worth it to you? If yes, hire her with extreme caution. If not, DO NOT HIRE! Be very clear about your choices. These are your hiring decisions. I can't say this enough. **You play a role in what type of business you're creating.** What are you saying yes to? What are you saying no to?

Staffing is so important to your business. I am sure there are going to be times when you will think you're willing to hire anybody just to fill a chair. I warn you, the best decisions are not made when driven by emotions. Stop! Take a deep breath. Go back to your vision. Go back to your mission statement. Be very careful about what you're saying yes to.

Reviews

When you have good reviews you won't need to look for staff. Artists will come to you asking to work there. They will seek you out to be cast for the leading role in your next film. When you have good reviews you won't need to look for clients. Clients will come running to you. Your audience will be waiting for the sequel.

Clients are always listening to what people are saying and watching what your staff is doing. When someone mentions your business or gives someone a business card they are doing a commercial or a promotion for your show. Based on the commercial the viewers are making a choice about whether to tune in or not. They will be sure to be home for this week's episode. That's equivalent to clients having regularly scheduled appointments.

You have some say about how you edit your script. This means you can change the way you do business. Unfortunately, you don't have any control over the reviews of your show. You may ask, "Who gives the reviews?" Your clients give reviews whenever your business is mentioned. Your staff gives reviews whenever they mention where they work. Just because they don't say anything to you doesn't mean they agree with what's going on in your business. Remember that bad news travels fast. Let's give them plenty of great news to spread! Word of mouth advertisement is the best free advertisement you're going to get. Many businesses have profited based on that alone.

Chapter 5
Recasting
Staffing Separation: Termination and Resignation

Here's the scenario. One of your lead characters hands in her resignation. You see her as an asset. She has a huge fan base. She generates a great deal of revenue. What should you do?

Take a deep breath. Explain to her how much you value her role on the team. Ask her if she has a moment to meet with you. When she agrees, be willing to actively listen. Ask her why she's leaving. Listen. Her response is that she has been offered a better opportunity. DO NOT SPEAK! Fully absorb the details involved in the other opportunity. Listen intently to why she's moving on. This is a great time for you to learn some things about yourself. That's right! It's time to learn about YOU! Take a moment to reflect. Be honest. Be open to what you will discover.

The original character in your script may have starred in the very first film you ever produced. She may have even been cast in the sequel. Now she's been type cast. She has grown as much as she can in that genre. She wants to be considered for other types of roles. It's time to hone her skills some more. It's time to take them to the next level.

In other words, she may have started out with you when you opened the doors to your business. She helped to give life to your vision. She has grown as much as she can in your salon. Her goals were a great compliment to your goals. They worked beautifully together. It's time to venture out into some other areas. It's time for her to use those gifts to bless others. There is a new dynamic to her partnership with you. It's time for you to support her growth outside of your business. It's time for you to support her as an individual.

She now has another assignment. When you try to hold her back, you are standing in the way of your blessings and hers. Do you really want to carry the burden of standing in the way of her greatness? Stay open to the possibilities of what's to come. Focus on the positive experiences and you'll attract more positive things and people in your life. Celebrate the good energy she brought into your business.

Take time to look within the walls of your soul. Do you want her to stay due to your own fears? Are you afraid that you won't find another actor that will act with such conviction? Are you afraid that your business will lose money? If so, do you know how much power you are giving to one individual? Remember, you created the last script. It was a success. Are you afraid to write another? The power lies within you. Ask yourself if there is anything you are willing to offer that will create a win for your business and a win for her. If the answer is yes, make the offer. If you're not sure, sleep on it. Hopefully, she's given you two weeks notice and you have time to find a resolution.

Be honest. If leaving is really a great opportunity for her to grow and you can't offer that, bless her by letting go. Wish her well in her endeavors. Let her know that your door is open to her if she needs you. Thank God for the gifts she brought to your business. Let her go gracefully. Honor her growth. I promise you, you will grow from the experience. What are you saying yes to? You're saying yes to new and exciting things in your life! Look forward to it. Get excited about it before it even happens.

A True Recasting Story

I met a talented young lady named Shante. She was an assistant in the salon I was managing. I literally watched her grow up. She was about 15 or 16 years old when we met. I remember her prom and all of those fascinating phases of becoming a woman. She was studying Cosmetology at the Vocational Center in a local high school. I watched her grow from Shampoo Assistant into Hairstylist. I knew that the time would come for her to go. I clearly remember the day that she told me she was leaving.

When she gave me the news, I congratulated her. What I didn't know was that the salon owner, Miki had also congratulated her. Miki and I hadn't had a chance to communicate how we felt about Shante's separation from the team with each other. I guess you can say that we're woven from the same cloth. Miki and I have a strong working relationship. Most importantly, Miki and I have very similar beliefs in how God works. We both knew the owner of the salon she was going to. We knew that it was time. We understood that this phase of her journey with us in this capacity had come to an end. We also knew that she had plenty more to learn. Many of these lessons were available at the salon she was going to.

The funny thing is Shante had expected a very different response from the one she received. She interpreted our "congratulations" as an "I'm glad you're leaving." Unbeknownst to us we had hurt poor Shante's feelings. When we became aware of it, we explained to her that although we would miss working with her, we were really excited about her growth opportunities.

Needless to say, it was one of the best moves she made. I'm proud to say that Shante has had an enormous amount of growth. That move pushed her to the next level. It was important for her to step away from what was comfortable and familiar. Shante not only spread her wings. Shante is flying to new heights as we speak. She is now the proud owner of a beautiful salon. She has built an extremely supportive clientele. She is well on her way to building a fabulous design team. This is just one of many success stories of people moving onward and upward without any hard feelings.

Letting Go and Moving On

Whenever a staff member hands in a resignation, take a deep breath and assess the situation. Sometimes a person's desire to leave on her own is a tremendous weight off your shoulder. You may have been getting ready to fire her anyway. Thank her for saving you the trouble. Be sure to thank her quietly in the privacy of your own thoughts.

Ignoring the fact that a team member's behavior is totally out of line with your business model will not make the situation go away. You play a role in what type of business you are creating. It's your vision that's being compromised. What are you saying yes to? The situation won't change on its own. You must address it.

Let's use an example. Christine has missed the last two mandatory staff meetings. She has only been on time for work once within the past month. When Christine gets there, the energy of the team depreciates. She has the audacity to bring her personal drama to work. Her clientele is slowly dwindling and she thinks it's your fault. Helloooo! That's costing you money!

What is avoiding the reality that a problem exists really costing you? It's costing you time, energy, frustration and possibly the respect of the rest of your team. What message are you sending to the rest of your staff? How is it affecting the team morale? Is this what you signed up for? Is this how you want to manage your business? When you decided to ignore the signs, what did you say yes to? You said yes to compromising your vision. You said yes to throwing money right out of the salon doors. You told your team Christine's personal drama and Christine's personal needs are more important than theirs.

Making A Clean Break

It is important to create a smooth transition with no hard feelings. When an artist is leaving the cast please give her access to her client files. Respectfully give her the opportunity to contact the clients that she primarily serviced. It is appropriate for you to also send letters to let the clients know how much you appreciate their business and that your current team will be happy to continue to service them.

What are you losing by giving her the right to communicate with her clients? I'll tell you what you're losing! Absolutely nothing! But you have plenty to gain. Having an attitude of abundance leads to a life of abundance. Move on. Put your energy into supporting your vision for the business. Use your energy to help nurture the next person on your path.

So we've experienced the loss of two artists. Don't fret. You have sample interview questions in chapter (4) four. Stay focused on the vision. Let's start interviewing. We have two positions to fill. Now get busy working towards auditioning new cast members.

Chapter 6
Show Me The Money

We all want to know how we're going to be compensated. There is no way to avoid this conversation. Of course we'd all like to ensure that our staff is compensated well for efforts. As a business owner, you need to be compensated also. Be careful not to focus solely on your staffing needs and forget about minding your business. If your business needs are not met, your business will eventually close.

Remember that all compensation agreements are personal and confidential.

Commission

Commission is a good way to balance your budget. There are several commission options. One way is to meet with your artist and agree on a "set percentage" based on her productivity. For example: The artist has an established client base. She is a huge contributor to the salon's bottom line. It may be a good idea to negotiate a reasonable flat rate. Her commission is the same regardless of how much revenue she generates each week.

Another option is a sliding scale. That means the commission percentage fluctuates based on the artist's weekly productivity. For example: If the artist is not consistently busy, you may want to use a sliding scale. When her production increases, pay her a higher rate of commission. When her productivity is low, her rate of percentage decreases.
This scale can be based on weekly or bi-weekly sales. This depends on when the payroll is processed.

I'll share one more option. Pay a higher rate of commission but the artist is responsible for purchasing her own products. For example: Pay her 70% commission. Unlike booth renting, all of her transactions are conducted through the front desk. The salon earns more than you would if she were renting a booth. However it reduces your inventory expenses.

Advantages:
- Greater income potential
- Consistent policies and procedures
- Greater team building opportunity
- Product consistency
- Better quality control
- Consistent pricing structure
- Consistent business hours
- Makes branding your business more accessible
- Increase opportunities to offer benefits
- More income the artists generates, the more revenue the business makes
- Encourages staff to be more engaged in the business

Disadvantages:
- Payroll responsibilities
- Income tax responsibilities
- Inventory tracking

Booth Rental

With booth renting, the salon owner typically charges a weekly rate for using a space within her business. It offers more financial rewards for the artist. In most cases, the artist creates her own business hours, purchases her own products and establishes her own pricing, etc. This is not an ideal situation for artists who have recently graduated from cosmetology school. It is designed for artist with an established clientele.

There are many booth rental success stories. You may find this more ideal for your business model. Consider the pros and cons to managing a booth rental salon. The name on the marquis is a representation of you and your business.

I recommend the same screening process in chapter (4) four when choosing the artists to whom you lease a space. Take the time to learn about the person you are inviting into your business. I also suggest scripting a lease agreement that honors your vision. Manage the booths with consistent policies to have quality control and some influence over your business reputation

<u>Advantages:</u>
- Minimal inventory expense
- No payroll responsibilities
- Reduced income tax responsibilities
-

<u>Disadvantages:</u>
- Limited income potential for the business
- Business expenses may increase when stylists use more water and electricity
- Artist functions as her own business entity with her own guidelines
- Inconsistent pricing structure
- Product inconsistency
- Less quality control
- Reduced team building opportunities

Transition from Booth Rental to Commission

If you currently have a Booth Rental salon and would like to transition into commission you could honor your current agreement with the existing staff. I would suggest, however, adjusting some of the current guidelines as it relates to the perception of your business. For example, set more boundaries for the hours of operation. You may want to make changes on the rent. Possibly give them the option of switching to commission as well. Present an attractive package. Of course you will want to fully analyze your current situation before making any changes. Weigh all of your options to determine what's going to be in the best interest of your business.

As you hire new staff, bring them in as commission artists. A sliding scale is always a great option to create a win for both you and the stylists. Develop a system for them to get a greater percentage on the weeks they generate more income. That gives them the incentive to earn more. It also helps to avoid paying out more than you can afford. This is especially good for new stylists who are building their clientele. What is the benefit to the business if you pay a high commission to someone that is not bringing in much income? It can possibly put your business in the red. My guess is that you didn't go into business to go out of business. Your rent or mortgage is still the same whether you make money or not. You must consider your overhead. You still have operating expenses such as water, electricity taxes, insurance etc. Meet with a financial advisor to determine what you can really afford to offer. The doors need to remain open in order to stay in business.

Salary

You may want to pay a salary or hourly wage for new artists fresh out of cosmetology school. This gives them the opportunity to earn an income while they build a clientele. One of their roles would be to assist the stylists that are busy. This provides an opportunity to learn from more seasoned teammates. It also gives her a chance to build a rapport with the clients. The learning that takes place in this role is invaluable. It's not only a very humbling experience, but gives her the chance to get life experience that isn't available in cosmetology school.

Establishing A Clientele

There are many ways to build a clientele. The salon owner is primarily responsible for marketing the business. However, it is also very important for the team to take ownership of this piece as well. The more energy a stylist/an artist puts into establishing clientele the more she will appreciate it. It also prepares her to be a better businessperson.

Client retention is huge. Train the team to schedule the client's next appointment prior to the client leaving the salon. The client is more likely to honor this appointment. Take control of the situation. If the client wants to call back to reschedule she's not likely to call by next week. If this client has a really busy schedule, she will easily get too busy to come in. Create an environment that encourages regular appointments as part of her lifestyle.

Develop a regimen for her services. Make recommendations for the next visit based on what the client needs in terms of care as well as what she says she wants. Be the expert. Write a prescription for her hair care needs.

Example: Let's look at Ms. Smith. Ms. Smith has relaxed hair. She gets her hair relaxed every 8 weeks. What does she need between now and then? She needs regular conditioning treatments. Her ends need to be trimmed regularly. She needs color to cover her gray. She also needs color to enhance her natural color. However, she says she doesn't want color so recommend a clear gloss to enhance the shine. Let's create a 9-week plan for Ms. Smith.

9 WEEK SERVICE PLAN

Week 1	Relaxer and trim
Week 3	Hair color, eyebrow color, eyebrow wax, moisturizing treatment
Week 5	Specialty set
Week 7	Protein treatment to prepare her hair for chemical service on the next visit. This is preventive maintenance to promote healthy hair. We want to protect the hair from chemical use as well as exposure to environmental elements such as sun and wind.
Week 9	It's time for a relaxer!

This prevents processing a ticket for a shampoo and style only. Teach your team to up-sell every chance she gets. This increases the average ticket. This increases the revenue for the week for the stylist and the business. When the client is accustomed to getting regular conditioning treatments, she will remind you that she needs the service. This is because you've set the expectation for it. You now have a regular 2-week client. Ask her for referrals. Reward her for the referrals. She'll send you more. Before you know it each stylist will have a fully committed schedule.

Please don't let her leave without:
1. A prescription or service plan for hair, skin and nails.
2. A scheduled appointment – clients are more likely to keep the appointment if they commit before they leave. She may have every intention of calling to schedule her next appointment. Everyone is busy these days. It's likely she'll forget to call back.
3. Business cards – ask for referrals.
4. A POSITIVE EXPERIENCE!

A few other things:

Cross selling is huge to growing your business. If you offer spa services, teach the stylists to recommend those services to every client they come in contact with and vice versa.

Build strong business alliances. Pass out business cards everywhere you go. Tell other business owners what you do. When you spend money with someone ask him or her to spend money with you.

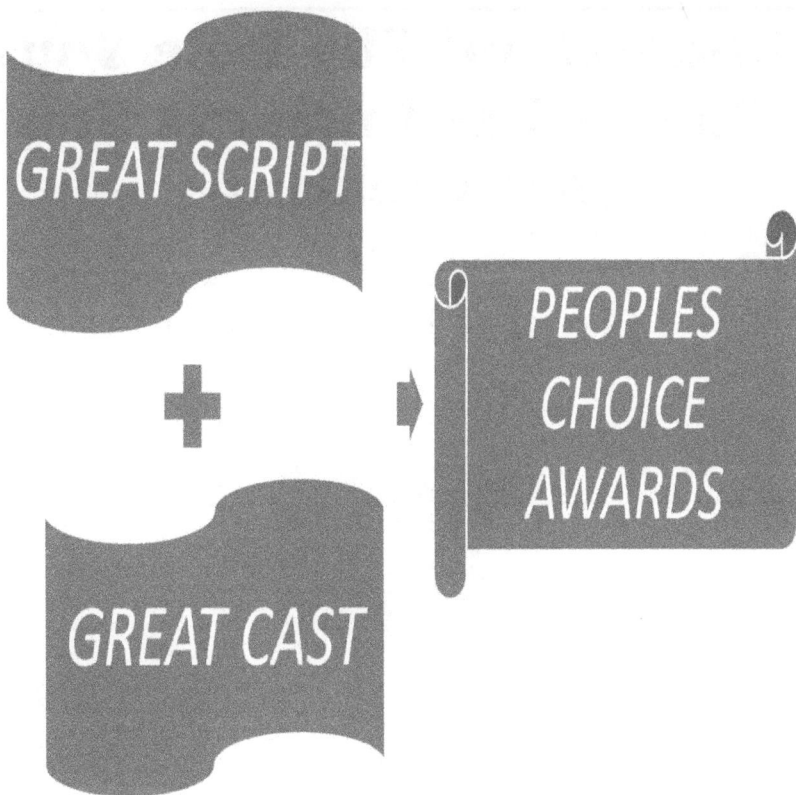

GREAT SCRIPT + GREAT CAST → PEOPLES CHOICE AWARDS

"The People's Choice For Salon of the Year Goes to...."

Understand The Role You Play In The Business You Are Creating And Hold The Vision

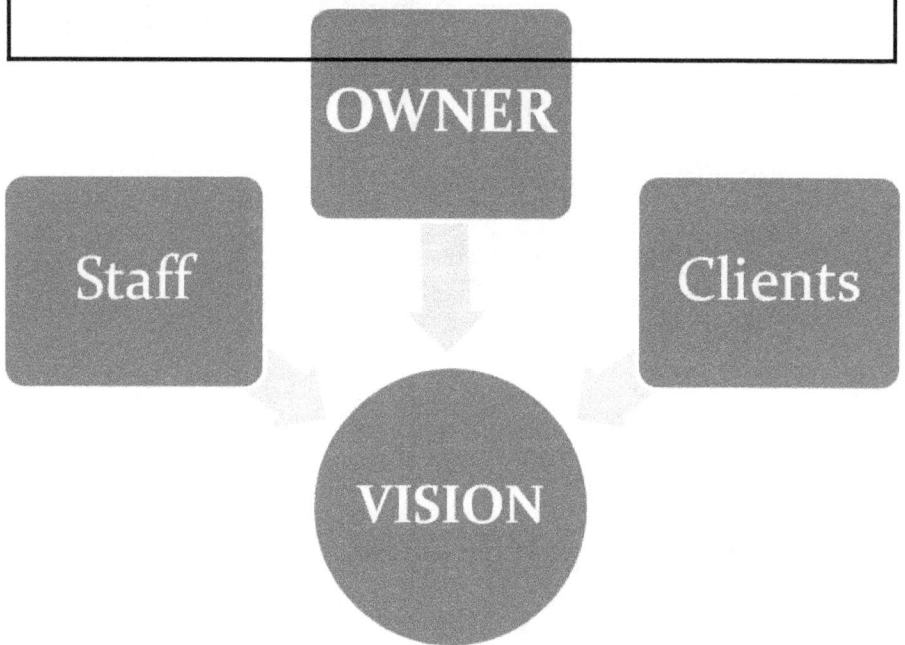

OWNER

Staff

Clients

VISION

Epilogue

Before I go, there are a few reminders. We are in the people business. We provide services for clients who have lives outside of our salon. Honor the client's time. Treat them as a whole person, not your 5 o'clock appointment. If you listen carefully to your clients, they will tell you exactly what they want. If you create a way to give them what they want while staying true to your vision, your business will grow.

Yes, it's your business. However, you must remember you're not in business by yourself. Treat your staff with respect. Take time to listen to what each stylist/artist wants and needs from you. Take time to train her. Support her in achieving her goals. Be open to new ideas and concepts they want to share. Everyday we have an opportunity to learn something new. God may have sent her to teach you something. It's a reciprocal process.

I am sure you have already invested an enormous amount of money in the salon. You've invested money into salon furniture, equipment, products and marketing. Don't you want a return on your investment? Invest your time and energy into redefining your vision as needed. Invest in the time it takes to set boundaries for your business. Invest in the time it takes to get your team on board. Educate them about the benefits of holding the vision. Show them how they benefit from holding the vision as well. Get them engaged in the process of reshaping your business.

It's your responsibility to partner with her. You are in this together. Be sure to create a partnership that supports your business model. Be mindful of what you say yes to. Take care of your team in a way that promotes a healthy environment for your business. They will in turn take care of the clients.

Hold the vision. Start from where you are now. Understand the role you play in the business you are creating. Have the courage to make the changes you deem necessary. What you want will begin to take place. Say yes to your vision. Say yes to positive new beginnings. Say yes and create the business you want. I wish you well.

About the Author

Melanie Foote-Davis is a Life and Salon Coach, Consultant and Educator. She has a gentle, yet no-nonsense approach to maintaining professionalism in the beauty industry. She managed the salon team at one of the 200 fastest growing salons in the country, as selected by Salon Today Magazine. She's passionate about coaching salon owners and aspiring owners on how to grow their business to its full potential.

She is the creator of Power Behind The Chair and the founder of Live By Design Coaching & Consulting. She also designed a program for teen girls--ELANCE. ELANCE is an acronym for Exceptional Leadership Achieved thru Nurtured Cultural Experience.

Melanie facilitates workshops on self-esteem, relational aggression, and media literacy. She helps young girls with developing effective communication skills, defining boundaries and goal setting. She taught them to not only believe in dreams, but how to make dreams a reality. Melanie has used this passion to challenge many to maximize their potential professionally, personally, spiritually and financially.

www.MelanieFoote-Davis.com

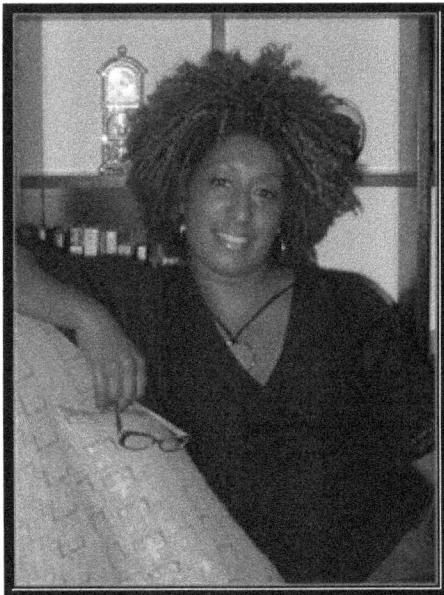

www.ingramcontent.com/pod-product-compliance
Lightning Source LLC
Chambersburg PA
CBHW021915190326
41519CB00008B/787